TAKE ACTION NOW

How to Live Your Dream in Less Than 3 Weeks

W9-CYB-319

EVAN MONEY

ISBN: 1-4392-1260-0
ISBN-13: 9781439212608

Visit www.booksurge.com to order additional copies.

I would like to thank Susan Money, my bride of eleven years. Thanks for continuously growing and for being my greatest "helpmeet."

Also, I would like to thank Jim Rohn, the "Greatest of All Time." Thank you for being the first person to help me on the road to self-improvement.

Lastly, thank you, John C. Maxwell, for putting the cookies on the lower shelf and for encouraging me to simply start writing.

CHAPTER 1

For those who are wondering, yes, my last name really is Money, and yes, my bride was very excited to "marry money." The challenge was, when we got married, I didn't have any. In fact, early on in our marriage, we were the ones holding up the line in the grocery store. Why? We didn't have the cash to pay for everything, so we had to put items back. Now our life is like a fairy tale, we live around the corner from Trump's new golf course in majestic Rancho Palos Verdes, California. We have full time staff to do our shopping now, we even hired a personal chef and my bride is a stay at home mom. To my bride's credit, she saw the dreamer in me and, most importantly, she learned to believe in her husband. Behind every man is a great woman, and sadly, most of the time it's not his wife. I'm truly blessed that the great woman behind me is my bride.

Secondly, you probably want to know what the story is behind the book's subtitle and promise: "Live Your Dreams in Less Than Three Weeks." Well, back in October of 2003, in Los Angeles where we live, I was driving my car and listening to some lame sports talk radio guy when, suddenly, I just got fed up. I said to myself, "I can do better than this guy."

Some of you have had the same experience, maybe not with radio, but with something else. However, instead of just thinking it, I TOOK ACTION, and in less than three weeks, I was "ON THE AIR" with an FM station and my own sports talk radio show. I was working in one of the largest radio markets, reaching over 15 million people. Wait. It gets better. I never went to broadcasting school, and I had never been on the radio before. I just took action and started living my dream. In less than six months, I moved to "prime time" on a #1 sports talk radio station, which at that time was Sporting News Radio.

> However, instead of just thinking it, I TOOK ACTION.

As amazing as this story is, it really is common-place if you look around. Have you ever heard of Joel Osteen? You know, the "smiling preacher" in Houston Texas? His ministry is shown all over the world to over 7 million people, and his church runs 30,000+ people every weekend. In fact, Osteen's congregation grew so big that he took over a sports arena (the former Compaq Center) and transformed it into a church. In case you didn't know, Joel never went to seminary or even graduated college.

How about Steven Spielberg, one of the greatest directors and producers of our time? Well, Steven never went to film school. That's right. He never went.

What's important to point out is that Joel Osteen, Steven Spielberg and I never got formal training, but we did get training. Osteen used to be the behind the scenes guy editing all his father's sermons. As Joel tells it, he would have to watch each sermon two or three times. So for ten years, he was getting his "training" by watching his dad.

Spielberg's story is a movie in itself. As a teenager he was at Universal Studios on the tram and just got really bored. To be fair, Universal Studios back then, some thirty or forty years ago, wasn't as cool as it is now.

Anyway, Steven got bored, snuck away from the tram, and found himself watching a real movie being filmed. He was mesmerized and ended up meeting a famous director who encouraged him to take action and pursue the film business.

Unlike most of you, he didn't just tell his friends, "Hey, check out what happened to me!" He *took action* and showed up the next day on the lot with his one suit and his dad's old briefcase with a candy bar in it. He strolled right up to the lot and walked in. He read the security guard's name tag, waved, and said, "Hey, Charlie." While others were in film school, listening to people who had never made a real movie before teach theory, Spielberg was learning from people who were actually making films. He did this day after day, and the rest, as they say, is history.

My training was the eleven years I spent in the world of sales. I was mainly in the area of wholesale distribution, so I was doing relationship selling before I even knew what that was. I just enjoyed talking to my customers and literally performing for them on the phone. I enjoyed being loud, funny, and encouraging (never obnoxious) by just having really high energy. It was the only way to keep me contained to my desk. When I got on the air I just did the same thing; I pretended I was talking to one of my customers. In fact, I made one of my customers a part of my show. I was living my dream and my customer got a chance to live one of his.

Speaking of dreams here is a list of my favorites that I have been able to live out. Now, I don't do this to impress you, but to impress upon you that you can do all this and more!

How would you like to:

Buy gas without looking at the price?

Snow ski and surf in the same day in ideal conditions?

Receive a standing ovation at Mann's Chinese theatre in Hollywood at a movie premiere?

Perform on a traveling skateboard trick team?

Be on the cover of multiple magazines?

Be a model that is featured in full-page advertisements?

Author two children's books?

Be a prime time sports talk radio host in Los Angeles?

Try out for a pro football team?

Be "on the field" during a NFL regular season game?

Rent out the Staples Center to play football with your friends ... then rent it out the next year to play basketball?

Get married in a different state or country every year?

Adopt a baby?

Own a multimillion-dollar extreme sports enterprise that you started with zero capitol or investors?

Create your own charity?

Own a custom, one of kind sports car featured in auto magazines?

Have personal relationships with pro football players who interact with you during the game and touchdown celebrations?

Make your own movie?

Be in world-class shape with a single digit body fat?

Have your wife be a full-time mom?

Hire a personal nanny/ assistant for your wife?

Hire a personal chef?

Live in the neighborhood you and your wife dreamt about when you first got married?

The size of your dream is totally relative. A big dream to one person may be small to another, but the fact is—you have a dream. I'm going to take you from having a dream to living your dream, some in less than three weeks! Are you ready?

"Yeah right!" you say. "This is just another 'pump you up, Motivational, New Age, Name it and Claim it' book," I hear you saying. Believe me, I understand your skepticism. I used to think the same way! But that is the real key, I don't think like that anymore, and that is why I have been blessed to be able to live my dreams. You are in life exactly where you should be because of the way you think.

Now, you're going to tell me all the reasons why you can't or haven't been able to make your dreams come true, right? You can say, "I had this happen to me" or "my childhood was traumatic." Look, all great people had to overcome the limitations put on them by others:

> You are in life exactly where you should be because of the way you think.

ALBERT EINSTEIN: His teachers said he was slow!

THOMAS EDISON: He was called a day dreamer in school; in fact, his Mom took him out of school and taught him at home.

WALT DISNEY: Over one hundred bankers said no to his dream of Disneyland. This was after he was a huge success and many of his cartoon characters were household names. He tried to convince his good friend Art Linkletter to buy up the surrounding property of the park because Walt knew hotels of all kinds would be built there. Even his good buddy Art could not see the vision. (As of this writing, Art Linkletter is still alive, and he would be a multi-billionaire today if he had taken Walt's advice.)

> "All our dreams can come true if we have the courage to pursue them." *Walt Disney*

So Walt *took action* and sold his mansion in Palm Springs to use as seed money for the project. Then, low and behold, a new phenomenon called "television" started taking off, and Walt jumped at the chance to have his own show! And guess what it was called? Disneyland. Walt used all the proceeds from the show to fund the Disneyland park. As they say, the rest is history!

I think that Walt's greatest quote is "All our dreams can come true if we have the courage to pursue them."

MICHAEL JORDAN: Michael Jordan didn't make the varsity basketball team. Think about it—the greatest basketball player of all time didn't make the team. He said that after he was cut, he went home and cried. Have you ever been there? I have! After he collected himself, he made a choice to get better and practiced and practiced. He even hung on the monkey bars to try to stretch himself. The result? He made the high school varsity team and then went on to a great college career punctuated by his famous game winning jump shot in the1982 NCAA Championship game. From there, he went on to the pros, and well, you know the story.

ROWDY GAINES: The three time Gold medalist in the 1984 Olympics was diagnosed with GUILLIAN-BARRE SYSDROME in 1991. He was told he would die or never walk again even if he did survive.

Not only did he survive, but he won two masters' swim titles and even qualified for the 1996 Olympic team at thirty-five years old. Now, he is no Michael Phelps, but three gold medals are awesome, plus making the team at age 35. Now that is living your dream!

OPRAH WINFREY: Born in podunk, Mississippi, to a poor, teenaged, single mother, money was tight, so Oprah had to wear dresses made of potato sacks. She was raped and molested at the age of nine by her cousin, uncle, and a family friend. At fourteen, she ran away from home to live on the streets. She got pregnant and gave birth to a son who died in infancy.

Now, she is the most powerful and most respected woman on the planet. She was the first African-American billionaire, and her philanthropy and charitable givings are huge!

JOSEPH: Back in Biblical times, people didn't have last names, but Joseph's story is much different from all the others. Born to a wealthy family, he was the youngest of twelve sons. He was his father's favorite son, so much so, that he was a given a spectacular coat. Joseph was also a bit bold, and he would share his dreams with his brothers.

After awhile, his brothers were fed up with him and decided to just kill him. As luck would have it, a few of his brothers talked the others out of killing him and just sold him into slavery instead!

Thus began Joseph's journey. He got out of slavery only later to be framed and sent to jail. After helping one of Pharaoh's assistants get out of jail and restoring the assistant to his key position, Joseph sat for years in prison "building character" as they say.

One day, Joseph was able to help the Pharaoh himself, and in less than twenty-four hours, he was the second most powerful person on the planet! A few years later, all eleven of his brothers came to him not recognizing him and bowed to him, begging for food and supplies. Here is the best part—Joseph forgave them all. "When you rise above your limitations, you can help others do the same."-Evan Money

> "When you rise above your limitations, you can help others do the same."-*Evan Money*

There is a great quote by Marianne Williamson that explains so well the concept of rising above your limitations:

> "Our deepest fear is not that we are inadequate. Our deepest fear is that we are powerful beyond measure. It is our light, not our darkness that most frightens us. Your playing small does not serve the world. There is nothing enlightened about shrinking so that other people won't feel insecure around you. We are all meant to shine as children do. It's not just in some of us; it is

in everyone. And as we let our own lights shine, we unconsciously give other people permission to do the same. As we are liberated from our own fear, our presence automatically liberates others."

What's the worst thing that could happen if you pursue your dream and don't achieve it? You could be where you are now!

Now, allow me to show you how to live your dreams, some in less than three weeks.

There are five KEYS you will need to unlock the doors that stand between you and all your dreams. Just like a real key, each key has to be cut and then polished to work properly. Now for some of you, these cuts may need to be deeper in some areas and less in others. In fact, you may already have some of these cuts in your key. Just like with a real key, the more you use it, the better it works, so don't miss the chance to improve on what you already have. The Greek philosopher Plato said, "The greater part

> What's the worst thing that could happen if you pursue your dream and don't achieve it? You could be where you are now!

of instruction is being reminded of things you already know."

The 5 Keys are:

1. Forgiveness

2. Association

3. Belief

4. Action

5. Today

Let's get started. There are action steps on the next page to help you even further. These steps will be at the end of every chapter to guide you along so that you can live your dreams even faster.

TAKE ACTION NOW!

#1. Get a pen, and write a dream or a few dreams right here in this book that you really want to live.

→ Residual Income.

→ Travel to all continents.

→ Build an amazing home with a great kitchen

#2. Write down the BIG DREAM you have that you think will never come true regardless of your self-imposed limitations.

Create Residual income/wealth

#3. Take a moment to think: When you're living those dreams, what will your lifestyle be like? Where will you live? What will you be driving? What clothes will you be wearing? What sporting or other events will you be attending?

Easy going, In more than (1) places, A sweet work van w/ TV's and a casual vehicle, something comfy but professional, my own.

KEY #1 FORGIVENESS

CHAPTER 2

What makes Joseph's story in chapter 1 so powerful is that Joseph forgave his bothers. Can you imagine how bitter and resentful most of you would be if anyone, let alone your own family, did those things that Joseph's family did to him?

Now some of you can't relate to Joseph, but you can relate to Oprah. The interesting thing is I have seen people spiral off into depression over much smaller things. So the degree of hurt that someone or a group of people have caused you to experience is irrelevant. The real question is what you're going to do with that hurt.

You can choose to hold on to the hurt, the hatred, the bitterness, and the resentment all you want. But as you have discovered, the only person it hurts is you. You can't compartmentalize unforgiveness and bitterness.

> You can't compartmentalize unforgiveness and bitterness.

Guys, in particular, are famous for being able to compartmentalize and just go into another room and be totally fine and enjoy a football game, even though they bounced a rent check or just had a fight with their wife. But you can't compartmentalize your anger and resentment. It's like standing in line next to a smoker. It just permeates the smoker's whole body. It's so disgusting. Have you ever stood next to someone who partied the night before and drank way too much? The drinker's body tries to detox itself by releasing all the alcohol he consumed through his pores. When you stand next to this person, they just reek! It's the same with resentment and bitterness. It permeates your whole body and spirit, and it affects everything you do in a negative way.

A doctor friend of mine told me about a lady he met in San Diego that told her story of resentment and unforgiveness; the hurt this woman went through was unbelievable. On her wedding night, her husband cheated on her with one of her bridesmaids! Can you imagine that? Think of the betrayal this woman felt from her husband and her so-called friend. She carried the resentment for over ten years.

She ended up getting terminal, inoperable cancer. The blessing of that diagnosis forced her to sit down and rethink her life. She turned to alternative medicine, and she was told to forgive her husband and the bridesmaid.

Finally, after ten years, she realized all the hate and anger was hurting her and she decided to just cleanse herself and forgive everyone. The great thing was that six months later, she was cancer free! The doctors were unable to find the cancer on any scans or tests.

Do you see what I mean when I say the only person who gets hurt from unforgiveness is you? The worst part about all this is the person who hurt you feels fine. They may not even know they hurt you, or if they do, they don't care! DAWN

Let me share with you a personal story: My wife and I had a chance to tear down our old house and build a custom home. Our original lot was so big we did the normal Southern California thing and built three houses on the property and decided to keep one for ourselves. Custom-built and designed for our family, it was a real dream come true. The challenge was I picked the wrong contractor, and to make matters worse, I made him my partner in the whole deal. Little did I know until it was too late that I made a bad choice. This guy was so unaccountable, so two-faced, so inept, it's impossible to describe what we went through. The worst part was I had so much anger and resentment toward this guy that I was unable to enjoy the house. Every time I looked at it, all I could see was the unfinished work that he promised to do and all the corners he cut and all the leaks, etc. I couldn't let it go.

We didn't live in that house for more than a year, but we decided to keep it and rent it. Even then, every time I heard the guy's name or his wife called about some paperwork that got screwed up, all these feelings would come flooding back, and I would get upset all over again.

Finally one Sunday, I was sitting on the couch watching Joel Osteen because I had just read one of his books and I wanted to see what he was all about. Guess what Joel's message was? That's right, forgiveness. I couldn't move; I was glued to my chair. He told me all the things I just told you about forgiveness but in his "smiley preacher" way. I finally had enough and I forgave that contractor right then and there. But it gets better.

Then, Joel preached that after I forgave the contractor, I needed to pray for that guy, pray for blessings for him. "Wait a minute!" I thought. I said to myself, "I'll forgive him, but I'm not praying for him." Some of you know exactly what I'm talking about. Deep down you know when you have not really forgiven someone, and deep down, I knew I had not totally forgiven this guy.

It took me about six more months to finally release all the anger, all the hatred, and really forgive that guy. I have prayed for blessings for that man a few times. Now, the resentment is totally gone. I no longer have any ill feelings towards him. Now don't get me wrong. I haven't called him and invited him over for dinner, but if I did ever see him, I would not look upon him with hatred. In fact, I might actually thank him because he helped me grow personally.

Similar to what Joseph did, he summed up what his brothers did when he said, "What you meant for harm, God meant for good." Listen, you don't need to go to church or "get religion" or watch Joel Osteen to forgive someone. You don't need New Age or Old Age or some Guru to forgive someone. You just forgive them. You just decide enough is enough!

> "What you meant for harm, God meant for good."

I know what you're thinking: "It would be nice to forgive them but … You don't know how bad they hurt me …" You're right. I don't know, but I do know what is really hurting you is that you're still carrying around all the anger and resentment. It's like poison in your veins, destroying everything around you. Let me put it this way. You will never live your dreams until you learn to forgive. Sure you may have some cool stuff happen to you, but deep down, you will still have this nagging emptiness until you can completely forgive the people who have hurt you.

> You will never live your dreams until you learn to forgive.

Once you forgive, you can begin to heal and move forward in your life.

Listen, what's done is done! You can't unscramble eggs. All these silly little sayings are actually true! Think about it. All you have is now. You can be bitter or you can choose to be better. You can choose to break through the barriers of unforgiveness that are keeping you from living your dreams.

Who do you need to forgive? Your son, your daughter, mother, father? Family friend or co-worker ? Who is it you still have anger and resentment towards? Are you a mother who had a son or daughter killed by a drunk driver or someone else? Do I understand you pain? I don't, but Mary does.

Mary's son was gunned down by a ruthless gang member. If anyone deserved to be angry, it was Mary. But the anger started to poison her, and she could tell it would destroy her unless she *TOOK ACTION*.

As part of her grief counseling, Mary visited the young man who killed her son. If you have ever visited anyone in jail before you know how a visitor, any visitor is a big deal. The young man had no clue who she was. In fact, he only recognized her through her tears, but once he knew her, he was speechless. Mary left, but came back a few weeks later and then came back a few days later. Pretty soon, Mary came everyday and began to build a relationship with this young man. One year later, Mary was able to put her arms around that young man and say "I now consider this boy my son!"

> "Remember weak people can never forgive, forgiveness is an attribute of the strong." -*Gandhi*

Talk about forgiveness! WOW!

"Remember weak people can never forgive, forgiveness is an attribute of the strong." -Gandhi

Are you a son who needs to forgive his father? This was lesson I had to learn. It took me thirty years, but I did it. You see, I come from a normal dysfunctional family. My parents got divorced when I was four, and we stayed with mom during the week and with Dad on the weekend. My dad was a structural engineer for McDonald Douglass for 40 years. He spent all day at work finding what was wrong with everything. So it was "this is wrong, that is wrong, fix this, fix that, etc." Then, he would come home and do the same thing to my mom, my brother, and me.

Imagine bringing home a project for school and all your dad can say is "This is wrong. That's wrong. Fix this, and fix that." It got to the point that from ages nineteen through twenty-five I stopped speaking to him. Keep in mind I was only ten or so miles from his house, but I just had so much bitterness inside I just tried to bury it. You can imagine all the pain that caused. Similar to what the government tried to do with all the toxic waste they had in Niagara Falls back in the 1970's. You know what happened, the containers started to leak and people started getting sick, all because they tried to bury something instead of dealing with it.

Finally after a lot of personal growth books, CDs and seminars, it was on my heart to grow up and forgive my dad. I was convinced mostly by an old cassette tape I heard where the guy talked about how you need to look at your dad's dad to figure out what shaped him and then, if you could, go back to your grandfather's dad, etc. I did that, and I found out that my dad never had a dad, or a least one that was around for him. So what did he know? Nothing. Sure he could have read parenting books and gone to personal growth seminars, but he didn't.

I realized I could #1 Forgive my dad and #2 Love my dad because he is my dad. Think about it, your dad did one thing right. You're alive, aren't you? So you can at least be grateful for that regardless of the circumstances of conception. You are here reading this book, growing, and changing to be a better person so you can live your dreams.

> Think about it, your dad did one thing right. You're alive, aren't you?

Now, my dad's story doesn't have some fairy tale ending for all you cynical people out there. My dad is still the same old structural engineer; he finds fault in everything. So, yes I have forgiven him and yes I love him because he is my dad and we do visit from time to time with the kids. But

I'm not able to have any real conversation with him because we think so differently. If I share any of my business ideas or the projects I'm doing he just says "Well this is wrong; that's wrong, etc." But here is the thing, it's ok. I'm not going to change him. So when we do talk I just stick to football and we chit chat a little about the economy but that's it. That's all he is capable of. I would prefer a more dynamic relationship but that's not possible. So I just love him because he is my dad and I have no anger, resentment or anything anymore. I just know that my dad is like concrete, all mixed up and permanently set. Now, can God change him? YES! And if he does fantastic; but I'm not going to let unforgiveness destroy any relationship in my life! Don't let it destroy any of yours.

Now I did say this story didn't have a fairy tale ending, but I must share a bright spot that really was a confirmation and a blessing for me: My bride and I renew our vows in a different state or country every year, and I will elaborate on this more in upcoming chapters. For our ten-year anniversary, we decided to go all out and get a new custom-made dress, and we booked the same church we got married in the first time. We purchased catering, flowers, the whole meal deal. It was quite an education for me on how much everything costs; that is for sure. If you have a daughter, like me, start saving now!

Anyway, my bride and I decided to do a little video that we would show during the service about the past ten years. We each spoke in a few thirty-second clips about some of the things we do to keep our marriage special. Our goal was to inspire others to have a better marriage as well. As it turned out, we were shocked with the letters, e-mails, and calls from people who were really touched by it.

A few weeks later, my dad came to visit and he asked, "You know that video you did for the wedding?" I immediately braced myself for the "this is wrong; that's wrong" comments. Then he said, "You know, I really got a lot out of that." I was speechless and in shock. Could it be I was actually able to get through to my dad? For one brief moment in time, I had the feeling of what a real father-son relationship could be like. This event gave me confirmation that the skills and tools I was teaching had value. I mean, if my dad got something out if it, it had to be good! Like I said earlier, my dad is still the same negative and critical person but I love him because he is my dad and I'm so glad I chose to forgive him.

On a side note, it appears to me that many religious people are the most unwilling to forgive. They seem to have the hardest hearts. If you can relate, then think about how much the Lord has forgiven you, for everything you have ever done. Psalm 130:3 says, "O Lord, who would be able to stand if you kept a record of sins."[1]

> Are you ready to finally let it go and forgive someone right now?

Are you ready to finally let it go and forgive someone right now?

TAKE ACTION NOW!

#1. Who can you call, drive to see or e-mail right now in order to forgive them? Phone and face-to-face interactions are better, but e-mail or hand-written letters work wonders too.

#2. Do not do anything else until you forgive that person or persons. Without it, the rest of this book is worthless! If you're just that stubborn to ignore all your tears and churning inside and you refuse to forgive that person or persons, then simply stop reading and give this book to someone who wants to move ahead in life and is serious about living their dreams.

KEY #2 ASSOCIATION

CHAPTER 3

Association typically has a sense of negativity with most of us because we first heard it during our teen years. This is when most of our parents were preaching to us, forbidding us to hang out with certain people or ignoring the people we hung out with. This is when we first started noticing cliques and that the jocks hung with jocks and the druggies hung with druggies and the gangsters hung with gangsters, etc.

The funny thing is most people think association only applies to junior high and high school. The truth is it's one of the main aspects that prevent people from living their dreams. Here is a great example: Think of the five friends with whom you spend the most amount of time. You all make about the same amount of money each year. Isn't that interesting? Now, imagine if your five closest friends were all billionaires. Do you think that would affect you financially in a positive way? You bet it would.

Speaking of billionaires, Warren Buffett said: "It's better to hang out with people better than you. Pick out associates whose behavior is better than yours and you'll drift in that direction."

> "It's better to hang out with people better than you. Pick out associates whose behavior is better than yours and you'll drift in that direction."

Now, let's look at relationships. If you are divorced, how many divorced people do you hang around? Do you think if your five closest friends had dynamic marriages that your marriage would be better? You bet it would. I would go as far to say that association isn't just a big thing; it's everything! The books you read and the people you associate with will determine where you are in five years! Period.

> I would go as far to say that association isn't just a big thing; it's everything!

If you're the type of person who likes case studies and you're looking for more detailed proof about this, then read on. In the bestselling book *The Tipping Point,* the author discussed one of the most rigorous studies of this kind, the Colorado Adoption Project, was done in the mid-1970's. This test was done with 245 pregnant women who were about to give their children up for adoption. They followed the children to their new homes, giving them personality and intelligence tests throughout their childhood. They also gave the same tests to the adopted parents. They also did the same thing with 245 parents with biological children. The bottom line of all their findings was that environment plays a big, if not bigger role than heredity, in shaping personality and intelligence. The interesting thing is the environmental influence doesn't have a lot to do with parents. Some experts argued that the environmental influence that helps children become who they are, that shapes their character and personality, is their peer group.

I think the inner cities and corporate America are a great example of this. If the corporate culture is backstabbing, lying, and two-faced like most corporations, you get low productivity and low morale. It's infectious; like a virus, it spreads. Similar to the post office, after six months or so, the socialistic system of government work just sucks the life out of everyone. The same applies to the DMV. Need I say more?

Now, let's look at the inner city. It's the same kind of mental prison that sucks the life out of everyone.

Of course there are a few "flowers in the sidewalk" that are able to make it out of that environment, but for the most part, it's an endless cycle of welfare and fatherless children.

Association is just like a sharp knife. In the hands of a surgeon it saves lives, but in the hands of a psychopathic demented soul, it takes lives. Let's revisit corporate America, this time with a company that uses the power of association for great productivity.

The GORE Company, the maker of Gortex, purposely keeps the size of its plants small so that it can avoid the normal layers of management. A company associate was quoted as saying, "This is what you get when you have small teams, where everyone knows everybody. Peer pressure is so much more powerful than a concept of a boss. It is many, many times more powerful. People want to live up to what is expected of them."[2]

> Peer pressure is so much more powerful than a concept of a boss.

The corporate environment of GORE is high production, high trust, and high morale. People don't want to let each other down. It is as infectious as the low morale virus; however, the results of high morale are much more exciting.

It's the same in a high-end neighborhood. It's so amazing to experience it. In today's big city world, you can take a drive from the inner city to a high-end area in a few blocks, in some cases. You can literally witness the transformation before your eyes. In a high-end neighborhood, graffiti is not tolerated. If there is any vandalism, it's taken care of right away. Even renters in high-end neighborhoods still take care of things.

So the proof is there; who you hang out with and where you hang out will determine your actions to a large extent. So let's start with who we hang out with!

Negative people and Dream-stealers:

> A perfect example of this is Rudy's story. If you don't know the story of Rudy Ruettiger, I suggest you get the movie (*Rudy*) because it's a classic. Rudy had a dream of going to college and playing college football. The challenge was no one in his family ever went to college, plus, his grades were below average, and he was too small to play

college football. Rudy didn't want to go to just any college. He wanted to go to Notre Dame! Notre Dame is famous because not only is it a world-class football program, but you have to have extremely high academic records to get in. So, you can imagine how Rudy's parents and friends reacted to his dream. He was either made fun of or told to be realistic and just be happy and settle for less in life. All of the people around Rudy said this but one person.

Rudy had one friend who, on his birthday, gave him a Notre Dame jacket. After Rudy opened it and put it on, still in shock at the great gift, his friend looked him in the eye and said, "Rudy, you were born to wear that jacket." The next day that "one real friend" died on the job in a freak accident. It was this event that shook Rudy to his core and got him to *TAKE ACTION* and quit his job and head for Notre Dame.

Rudy's Dad met him at the bus stop to try to "talk some sense" into his son. He told him again to be realistic and that Ruettigers were not special. They were not made to go to college. Can you imagine that? Gee, thanks Dad for all your support.

Rudy didn't give up. He got on the bus and without spoiling the whole story (because I want you to watch the movie), he got into Notre Dame, he got on the football team, and he even played in a game. Rudy is still the only player in Notre Dame history to be carried off the field in victory. Not even Joe Montana or Nute Rockne, two of Notre Dames most legendary players, can claim that feat.

Life is too short to hang around negative people—even if it's family. Now I know this may be a hard one to take because it was hard for me to take. You may feel like you are obligated to hang out with your family. Don't do it! What if Rudy had listened to his family? Do you know who the most excited person was watching Rudy play at Notre Dame? His dad! The very same guy who tried to talk him out of living his dreams was his biggest cheerleader

> It's the same with your negative family; you owe it to them to distance yourself so you can live your dreams.

when he made it! It's the same with your negative family; you owe it to them to distance yourself so you can live your dreams. Why? Because when you do, like Rudy, it will set them free!

Listen, you don't have to move out of state and never talk to your family again. Just slowly distance yourself. In fact, a great way to do this is to limit the amount of time you spend with negative family members. Instead, every month, put it on your calendar to send them a handwritten card. Most of the time, they won't care that you don't come around as much if you send a nice card every month.

My wife and I had to do the same thing with our family. This is how I did it. I sat down with them and said, "Either shape up, or you will never see us or your grandchildren again." I don't recommend this approach unless it's really necessary. Now, I'm giving you the condensed version but because of their destructive behavior, I literally sat down with them in a coffee shop and told them to quit what they were doing, or they would not see us again.

Now, the best way to do this is not to tell the people what you're doing. It works a lot smoother that way. Listen, I know some of you ladies may be a little upset and you make think because I'm a guy I don't understand the dynamics of women's relationships or family relationships. I do understand. Let me suggest a great way to help you distance yourself from negative family members and friends so that you can live your dreams and set them free.

First off, let's start with friends. Make a list of the people who you notice are critical, negative, judgmental, and are dream-stealers. Once they are identified, you need to make a conscious effort to slowly distance yourself from them. So, if one of them calls and wants to chit chat, ladies (guys don't chit chat), you simply thank them for calling but say, "I have to run." Don't say, "I'll call you back." Don't say, "Call me later." Just say that you have to run. Then, you can simply drop a handwritten note or a card to that person. When your negative friends call and you are always busy or you don't hang out with them anymore, they'll get the idea. If you send cards, however, they know you care. It's part of life. People just fade away sometimes, even people we like. You're just consciously fading away.

Now, for family it's a little different. There are a lot of dynamics and issues with the children, etc. Of course, each situation is different. You may need to do what I did, or perhaps you can just limit the visits with family members. If you must spend the same amount of time, make sure to keep the conversation light and trivial. I understand the desire to share things with your relatives, but just don't do it. Make sure to share your dreams and goals with "real friends," and if you don't have any, then go find some. You don't need to build a dynamic friendship over many years. Just find someone you can share your dreams and ideas with who will encourage you. Once you have someone to share with, you won't feel so bottled up. When you get around the negative people, you can just keep it calm and light.

But what if the most negative person is your spouse or girlfriend/boyfriend? Listen, I understand, and without writing a whole marriage book, let me give the best of what I have learned as a pre-marital counselor and a marriage seminar teacher.

Let's start with the girlfriend/boyfriend. Typically, if you're asking me this question, you are in a long-term relationship and you're probably living with the person. The reality is that you really don't want to marry this person, but you don't want to be lonely either. You feel like you have

> Life is too short to settle, especially settling for a dream-stealer.

invested so much time in this relationship, so you are just cruising along. If you think I'm wrong, then you would have married this person already. My advice is to break up with this person right now. Life is too short to settle, especially settling for a dream-stealer. You're never going to live your dream in a cruising relationship. I can guarantee that.

Now for the people who are already married, you have some work to do. You got yourself into this mess, and you need to clean it up. Divorce is not an option unless there is physical abuse involving you or your children or infidelity. That's my stand. If the above mentioned is happening, then the few paragraphs here are not the answer. In the case of abuse, I would get you and the children as far away from that person as possible.

For those of you with just your normal, typical, crappy marriage where your spouse is overly critical and judgmental, I would suggest this: take responsibility and win them back! Most people with marriage issues always blame the other person, but the reality is your negative, dream-stealing spouse is acting this way because of you or at least partly because of you. First of all, if you *took action* from chapter 1, you would have already forgiven your spouse and told them so. Apologize for your behavior even if you have nothing to apologize about. Then, simply begin winning them over with your actions. For more help with this, I would strongly suggest the two best books on marriage ever written: *The Five Love Languages* by Dr. Gary Chapman and *Your Personality Tree* by Florence Littauer. Now, let's talk about where you live.

Here is another case study for you people who like details and dates. In the 1970's, Stanford University social sciences did a study where they created a mock prison in the basement of the university. The reason for the study was to see why prisons were such terrible places. Was it because the prisons were full of terrible people or because the environment was terrible? They recruited volunteers to be pretend prisoners and pretend guards. The experiment was to last two weeks, but they had to shut it down after only six days.

In the first two days, five "prisoners" had to be released because of hysterical breakdowns and extreme emotional depression. Many of the guards who were self-proclaimed pacifists turned in to cruel sadistic, hard-bitten disciplinarians. One guard said it was all a part of the whole atmosphere of terror they felt they had to have. One of the prisoner volunteers said emotionally it was a real prison he was in; it was no simulation. It was that powerful of an experience. The conclusion was that there are specific situations so powerful that they can overwhelm our inherent predispositions.[3]

As a resident of Los Angeles, I have seen firsthand how a neighborhood can shape people's lives. Even just a few blocks can make a world of difference where I'm from. In fact, one of the great charities I support is called World Impact (worldimpact.org). They have a camp in the Los Angeles mountains, only forty miles from Watts or any other famous Los Angeles ghetto. But it might as well be a galaxy away.

What they do is bring inner city families out for camp every summer. For most of these kids, it's the first time they have ever left a four block radius. They spend time in the mountains, fishing, swimming, playing paintball, and having all kinds of fun. You can guess what a huge impact it has on the kids and the parents. As supporters, my wife and I get letters all the time from the kids about how much they enjoyed it and how much their parents changed when they were there. Think about it. While at camp, the parents are in a safe environment surrounded by loving people who just want to give. There are no gang members, no police officers, no drunk and disorderly neighbors. There is just a peaceful, quiet environment for families to enjoy each other.

For most of you middle-class people this makes perfect sense, but you're missing how it applies to you. For this example, I'm assuming you want to break out of mediocrity and that you're ready to live your dreams. For a lot of you, this dream includes your dream home. Remember in the first chapter we talked about dreams being relative? For the inner city family who is on food stamps, etc., living in a middle-class home would be living their dream. But if you're in that middle-class home now and you are ready to take it to the next level, you need to watch your environment.

Here is what I suggest: take a drive to your dream neighborhood. For some, that's right on the beach; for others it's the penthouse of some posh high-rise community; for others, its acreage and space. Wherever it is, go there and look around. Look at the architecture, look at the people, and look at what they are wearing (or not wearing, for beach folks). Look at the cars that are in the neighborhood. Check out the nearby shops and restaurants. Listen to how people talk! Let it all soak in.

When you return to your middle-class home, you will start to notice a different feeling. You will notice the lower-end type of cars and all the minivans. You will notice the difference in the way people dress and how they carry themselves. Now, listen to how people talk. Most middle-class people talk about high gas prices, their car's gas mileage, benefit packages at work, and how expensive every-

> However, in the dream neighborhoods, they speak of opportunity, they speak of ownership, and they speak of philanthropy.

thing is. However, in the dream neighborhoods, they speak of opportunity, they speak of owner-ship, and they speak of philanthropy.

It's such a huge shift in mind-sets. But, if you spend all your time in your middle-class home you will never be able to experience the difference. Next, let's look at where you hang out.

Similar to the dream neighborhood vs. the mid-dle-class neighborhood, the language and dis-cussions will be much different at the country clubs and yacht clubs vs. the local sports bar or the neighborhood barbecue joint. If you want to break out of mediocrity and get to the next level, you need to look at where you hang out. By sim-ply choosing to put yourself in the proximity of wealthy people, you now give yourself a chance to make that key connection. Remember, it's not whom you know but who knows you. Put yourself in proximity with these people so that when you do talk to them and meet them, they will assume you "belong," so to speak.

"Ok, back up," you might say. "How can I get into that country club, or how can I get into that private party? There is no way!"

> The way you think right now has gotten you exactly where you are in life.

First off, you have to stop thinking this way. Change your thinking so you can change your life. The way you think right now has gotten you exactly where you are in life. For most of us, that's a hard one to swallow, but its true! Now, let's try it again. Here is a great way to get in proximity to wealthy, influential people.

Restaurants are a great place to be. No matter where you live, someone can tell you which restaurants are the high-end, big-time places to be. One option is to go to the bar and nurse a club soda and hang out for a few hours. Don't go in and get loaded and then make a fool of yourself! In fact, I highly recommend not having any alcohol at all so that you can be sharp and on your toes. Make sure to tip the bartender big. Order your club soda, and tip the guy ten or twenty dollars! I'm serious. The bartender will be happy and won't care if you are filling a stool, plus, most of the regulars will talk to the bartenders. As you start to frequent a place, you will be known as a "who's who" just by leaving a good tip.

If you are hung up on the ten or twenty dollars (most middle-class people are) just look how much you paid for a beer at the last game or club you went to and you didn't think twice. Plus, if you only buy one club soda, you're better off than buying three club sodas and only tipping a dollar each time. In fact, you're saving money by being a big tipper!

If you decide to go to the restaurant, just get an appetizer. Again, leave a good tip for the bartender, the waiter, and the waitresses. Also, tip the hostess or maître d'. As you continue to frequent the restaurant, you will be known and you can then get that good table that puts you next to the right person or key contact. For you stubborn, middle-class mind-set people, don't whine to me about how you can't afford to do this. You just spent the same money already this week on lattes, junk food, parking, sports betting and clothes you didn't need.

Here is one last suggestion on restaurants. I remember the staff members' names and forge personal relationships with them. In fact, at one high profile restaurant I frequent, one of the waiters is a very outspoken Christian man who loves to share his faith. So whenever I'm there, regardless if he is my waiter, I call him over and pray with him. Now I'm not doing this in some superficial way; I'm genuinely interested and care about these staff members. I don't hang out with them and invite them over to the house, but I make it a point to be an uplifting presence to them and a giver of good cheer. It is better to be a giver of cheer than a loser and taker, a middle-class selfish person who just wants to get ahead. When you combine being a good tipper with an uplifting attitude, you become a "who's who" in that restaurant.

> When you combine being a good tipper with an uplifting attitude, you become a "who's who" in that restaurant.

Another place of influence is the golf course. There are a lot of high-end public courses in any town. If you're not a big golfer, it does not matter. In fact, at most public courses, you can putt on the practice area for free. Just show up and putt around for a little while. You would be surprised who you run into. The key to this is not to be so focused on your putting, but rather whom you run into.

Lastly, the best place to meet and connect with wealthy people of influence is at charity events. The great thing is even if you donate a meager amount just once, you get on the charity mailing list. The goal for them is, of course, to get you to donate more at all the different events. Don't worry about the amount, just do your homework and figure out which charities fit the connections you are looking for. If you're a starving artist, Hollywood-type person and you need some connections, make a contribution to some of Steven Spielberg's charities or Brad Pitt and Angelina Jolie's. Just get on the list.

Some of the events may require you to buy a seat or a plate for a large amount that you don't have. It's ok. They always have one or two free events every year. The key again is to do your homework so that you end up at the right event. Lastly, let's look at recreation.

You can apply what I just shared with you to any recreation, so I won't go over that again. What I do want you to look at is the type of people you are around when you're just relaxing. Take your

> you may be holding yourself back by who you choose to compete with.

softball team, for example. If you're like me, you are competitive and you want to play and win. So sports are not an area where you want to connect or network. You just want to play and get some exercise. I understand, however, you may be holding yourself back by who you choose to compete with.

Let me share with you my recent flag football story: As you can imagine, association is a big thing for me. It is on the forefront of my mind and my radar constantly. With that in mind, I was frustrated with the lack of participation I was getting in trying to get a group of friends to play flag football. So I decided to form a team of my own and enter a league. I thought that at least I'd be guaranteed to play because the other teams would show up. I knew, however, that a lot of the guys who play in these leagues have major "father-son issues" and swelled egos. I figured our team would hold each other accountable and we could offset any negativity with our team spirit. Yea, right!

You can imagine what happened. As soon as we played one of these ego-ridden, trash talking, "I think I'm in the NFL" type teams, we started acting just like them. The worst offender, of course, was me! That situation was so powerful that it over-whelmed my beliefs and took over my actions.

This is a great example of why people need coach-ing and mentoring in their life. I knew better, yet I still went against my good judgment. It's a great asset to have a coach or a mentor to be there to remind you of things you already know and to help you make the best decision. This is why I suggest you check out www.lifecoach5.com. It's a great way to get world-class life coaching that you can afford now, while you're making the jump to the next financial level. I know it's a plug, but at least it wasn't a ten page infomercial.

There is one other part of association I want to cover, and that is deciding to grow up. Keep in mind that when I say "grow up," I do not mean giving up on your dreams and sit-ting in a cubicle. I do not mean "get realistic" and shrink your dreams to match the rest of the boring mediocre people. I do not mean that you should stop being an idealist and conform to the broken patterns of society that don't work. What I mean by growing up is realizing that if you really do

> Keep in mind that when I say "grow up," I do not mean giving up on your dreams and sitting in a cubicle.

want to make a difference and you do want to live your dreams, you have to make some changes.

Let me share with you a great illustration about this with a story from my youth: Some of you may not remember, but there was a band from England back in the 1980's called WHAM U.K. The lead singer was George Michael, who may sound familiar to many of you. The group was popular in England because of their "bad boy rebellion to the establishment" type songs. The group had lyrics like: "Hey, jerk. You work; This boy's got better things to do; I may not have a job but I have a good time." This is why a lot of you are rebelling from the cubical world in corporate America. "If this is what a job is about then forget it. I'll just go party," you say.

If you're reading this book, however, I think you're a little different. You realize that being irresponsible isn't the key to happiness. You have a dream, a goal, a purpose, and you are looking for it. But you know that your dream is not a part of the suit and tie, close-minded world of today. So, if you're still looking for that dream, I'll give you this quote: "Do what

> "Do what you have to until you find what you are meant to do!"

you have to until you find what you are meant to do!" We will come back to this, but let's get back to Wham for a moment.

Wham came to America, and the promoters wanted to go for a more metro look (before metro was invented), and they had their new, lame, fruity songs like "Wake Me up before you Go-Go." Their big promotion was "choose life," but it had nothing to do with abortion arguments.

When I first saw this, my friends and I tried to get shirts that said "choose death." You see, to us the "choose life" promotion was so lame that we had to rebel. We were not into promoting death or suicide, but the "choose life" challenge was so dumb because of the image they were selling. My only choice was to do the opposite. This is similar to a lot of you who are rebelling against your parents' world, but your rebellion isn't what you really want. You just don't want the lie they sold you, so a lot of you wear funky clothes that don't fit. Some of you don't wash your hair. You take a job that pays eight dollars an hour because you don't want to be a cubicle guy or gal. You have long-term relationships with people you know you won't marry. You don't want to be lonely, so you just keep going out wasting years.

You are afraid to get married because you think you will be conforming. Perhaps you really want a marriage to work, but you think if you get married, then you'll get a divorce like 75% of the people in the U.S. Let me give the best example of not selling out and making your dreams come true:

Walt Disney is the biggest visionary of our time. His impact has been felt for generations. He has brought us Disneyland, Disneyworld, movies, etc., but Walt realized that he had to play the part until he could call the shots. He appeared on television, with a suit and tie. He had corporate offices. They worked from nine to five! Disney didn't work these hours, but the structure was there.

But he never sold out. He realized he needed the financial backing and partners to make Disneyland happen, so he played the part until he could call the shots. Then Walt was of course "the man" and known as being somewhat eccentric. The basic rule is when you're broke and have no money, you're immature. When you're wealthy, you're eccentric.

Some of you are saying, "Well, I'm not looking to be the next Walt Disney. I don't want to be a founder, but I do want to make a difference." If this is the case, then what I learned from the book *Orbiting the Giant Hairball* will really help you.

It was written by a Hallmark executive who was frustrated with all the corporate garbage and politics that hindered what Hallmark was about, which was creating great greeting cards. His big thing in the book was he realized that containers contain! He is basically saying that you can't get mad at a container for doing what it was made to do, which is to contain.

Let me put it to you this way. I don't get frustrated at the medical profession or the customer service representative at the bank who doesn't understand common sense anymore. Containers contain. Just work around them. Sometimes you're stuck, like flying commercial. Flying commercial means that you are in the container, endless check-in lines, delayed flights, and missed flight connections. Grow up and quit complaining; that's what happens when you fly commercial. I see people get all bent out of shape over this stuff and a lot of the time the complaints come from people who fly regularly. It's like being a nun and going into a strip bar and complaining to the manager about the dress code! If you don't like it then rent a private plane or buy your own plane. I did! I rented a plane to fly the family to Vegas for a little get away trip; it was the greatest flying experience of my life. First off, the pilots carried our bags from the car to the plane. Get this: no security check, no strip search and I got to keep my water I was drinking. After we got all loaded up, the pilot asked "Are you ready to take off now, Mr. Money." It sure beats waiting in line for two hours at LAX. Now when I'm stuck flying commercial, I realize the commercial aviation container I'm getting in and I have a much better attitude.

O.K. Let's wrap this up and put it together. If you really want to make a difference, realize that the marketplace works like this: the more value you add, the more money you make. Look at Oprah— she adds a lot of value or perceived value, and she is a billionaire who has a lot of influence. Value is relative. What's valuable for you may be junk to others.

Look at custom cars; there is a multi-millionaire in my neighborhood who makes aftermarket high performance car parts. For some, that adds a lot of value to their cars and lives. This guy is very wealthy. You need to become more valuable if you are going to make more money to fund your dreams or ideas. Perhaps you want to create a new division at the company where you work. You need to become more valuable to the company so that you can gain influence to get your ideas acted upon. You don't become more valuable by playing video games or managing your fantasy football team!

> You don't become more valuable by playing video games or managing your fantasy football team!

The first step to adding value is to add value to yourself. Walk down to a department store and look in the full-length mirrors. Really look at yourself and ask, "Do others take me seriously? Better yet, do I take myself seriously?" I could fill a whole book on just this subject, so rather than writing another book, I encourage you to watch five episodes of the hit show on the cable channel TLC called *What Not to Wear*. The greatest advice I can give about self-image is to watch that show. Watch how people's self-image is transformed by a set of new clothes that fit. It's so amazing!

The best way I know to sum up this chapter is Proverbs 13:20: "He that walks with wise men shall be wise: but a companion of fools shall be destroyed."[4]

This passage really says it all. Ok, let's turn the page and get to our action steps so we can start making some progress!

TAKE ACTION NOW!

#1. What toxic relationships do you need to step away from?

#2. Make a decision to upgrade your associations and to limit the exposure to negative, critical, and dream-stealing friends and family.

#3. Go back and read the dreams you wrote down from chapter 1. Now, ask yourself the same lifestyle question as before and dwell on it for a moment. Where would you live? What clubs or organizations would you like to belong to? What is the kind of people you would like to be associating with?

KEY #3 BELIEF

CHAPTER 4

We all remember the hit movie *The Matrix*. The first movie was truly revolutionary in so many ways. Remember when Morpheus, who is played by Lawrence Fishbourne, is teaching NEO, played by Keanu Reeves, how the whole Matrix world works? As NEO progresses and begins to surpass his teacher, one of the others asks, "What is happening?" To this Morpheus calmly responds in a prophetic manner, "He is starting to believe."

A few years ago, Disney came out with arguably the best sports movie of all time: *Miracle*. It was about the 1980 U.S. Olympic hockey team. The movie was special to me in so many ways; one was because I can remember exactly where I was when team USA, a bunch of young nobodies beat the greatest hockey dynasty in Olympic history, the Russians.

For you movie buffs, what makes this movie so great, other than the fact that it's a true story, is the fact that the movie holds you spellbound even though you know the ending. In fact, even the people who worked on the film in postproduction, on sound and editing, said that even though they saw particular scenes hundreds of times, they were brought to tears every time. The movie ends with Kurt Russell doing a monologue as he plays the late Herb Brooks, and he says some of the most powerful words: "On one weekend, as America and the world watched, a group of remarkable men gave the nation what it needed most, a chance for one night not only to dream, but a chance once again, to believe!

> a chance for one night not only to dream, but a chance once again, to believe!

I get goose bumps every time I hear or even read these words!

The message of "believe" also transcends music, from country and western to alternative, to contemporary Christian and everything in-between. We all have our favorite style of music and we all have a "believe" type song in our iPod or our CD collection. Why? Because we all want to believe in something. In fact, we all want to believe in ourselves, but most of us never do!

> In fact, we all want to believe in ourselves, but most of us never do!

I'm the first to admit that having you just read this chapter will not give you lifelong belief in yourself, but it's a critical part of the process. If you're brought to tears like me every time you watch the movie *Miracle*, then that movie is part of the process also.

The only reason I was able to go from being in my car listening to some lame sports talk radio hosts, to being on the air with my own show in less than three weeks is because I believed! Think about it. I had no broadcasting experience or schooling, and I found myself sitting down with the big wig radio executives in one of the largest radio markets in the United States, selling them on why my show should be on the air. I had no idea how I was going to pull it off. I didn't read any radio books; I didn't even practice. All I knew was that I could do better than the guys who were on the air. I held on to that belief to get me through everything necessary to get on the air.

What's interesting about belief is that many of us have it in one area, but not in others. It's so easy to see potential in others, yet for some reason, we have a problem seeing it in ourselves.

Here is an example from a new angle: The owner of the custom car shop where I ordered my

Batmobile Tumbler from is a master at his craft. Yet it took him thirteen years to finally believe what was obvious to everyone else. He had a gift for restoring and painting cars. He was consistently doing it on the side for friends, and word of mouth spread as he went through career after career.

Finally, his wife was able help him break through. She believed and that is what pushed him over the edge to open his own shop and do cars full time! Now, of course, you need to get in line if you even want this guy to look at your car, let alone work on it. When he flew out here to go over the designs of my car, he told me the whole story of his success, and then he said the greatest thing. He said he doesn't work; he is doing what he loves. I'm adding that he is living his dream. In his case it was a thirteen-year journey. I'm sure he would have preferred the three week journey.

That's why I wrote this book, to help you make the process as short as you can from where you are now to living your dream. But the process is different for everyone. Some may be able to do it in twenty-four hours, others and hopefully not you, may take twenty-four years. Regardless, the

> the main thing is to live your dream instead of just having one.

main thing is to live your dream instead of just having one.

We have all heard people say "I have to see it to believe it." I personally think you have to "Believe it to see it." Belief is stronger than knowledge. In fact, it's stronger than anything really. Faith would be another way to more adequately describe belief. You have to believe to have faith right?

In fact, Jesus was always big on pointing out people's lack of faith. He was always encouraging his disciples to have more faith and to believe more.

Matthew 17:20 says: "Because of your lack of faith. I tell you with certainty, if you have faith like a grain of mustard seed, you can say to this mountain, 'Move from here to there,' and it will move, and nothing will be impossible for you. [5]

In Mark 9:23, he says, "If you can believe, all things are possible to him who believes." [6]

TAKE ACTION NOW!

#1. What are you truly passionate about? If you could get paid to do anything (forget being realistic), what would it be?

#2. What are you a natural at? What have other positive people said that you should do because you're such a natural at it?

#3. Go back and read the dreams you wrote down from chapter 1. Now, ask yourself the same lifestyle question as before and dwell on it for a moment. If you really believed, where would you want to live? What would you really want to be driving? What causes do you believe in that you could support financially?

WHERE DO YOUR BELIEFS COME FROM?

CHAPTER 5

Let's take a look at how we got some of our beliefs. This chapter will speak to you if you're a woman, and guys, don't skip it because it will help you to understand women better. Trust me. We all need as much help as we can get to understand women a little better.

For all my female readers out there don't get upset, I'm only partly kidding. I think with a little help, men truly can understand the opposite sex better. Also I want to point out that in this chapter it's not my intent to make broad assumptions about women. My goal is for you to relate in some way to the things I'm talking about. What is great about women is that they are more open to sharing things than men, so even if you don't relate you can share with someone who will. With that, let's dive right in.

Most ladies look at movie stars and say, "Wow! I wish I had hair like so and so," or "I wish I had so and so's life." Do you know what all the movie stars secretly wish? They wish they had your life sometimes. No way, come on. They wish they could walk down the street without the paparazzi following their every move! They wish they could go to the grocery store and not get mobbed! Funniest of all, they wish they could have a bad hair day!

Ladies, when you have a bad hair day, nobody cares but you. Movie stars don't have that luxury of a bad hair day. They can't go outside unless they look perfect. Otherwise, they are all over the tabloids with captions like "so and so goes on drug binge" or "so and so has a nervous breakdown." It's the ultimate paradox! You wish you were them and they wish they were you. Think about that for a moment.

> Ladies, when you have a bad hair day, nobody cares but you.

A famous marriage counselor told this story that involved being on an airplane with the Dallas Cowboys' cheerleaders. (For the single guys this would be one of the rare benefits to flying commercial.) To prove this exact self-image point to his friend, the marriage counselor did a survey with one of the ladies. He asked her to rank herself beauty wise from one to ten. He purposely picked the most outwardly beautiful and the obvious "ten," and here is what she said: "Oh no, I'm a seven. Michelle over there, she is a ten!" To most guys, this is mind-blowing. Most ladies think that everyone feels this way. Most women do think less of themselves than others perceive them. Why is that?

Well, women are bombarded with images from television, billboards, and magazines constantly, which say they are not beautiful unless they look perfect. However, looking like this is not reality. The images are airbrushed, so none of these images are real. The key, ladies, is to wake up! Wake up and stop buying the beauty lie. The outside doesn't make you beautiful. The inside does.

Ladies, you have all seen women that just light up a room. Many times, they don't have much or any make-up on, or you don't even notice because there's an inner beauty inside shinning through. I think deep down all women know this, but the beauty lie has been bombarding you and beating you down since you were a little girl. In order to stop living the beauty lie and live our dreams, we need to identify where the lie came from.

One of the main culprits is Barbie! An article from the *Atlanta Business Chronicle* says it all: "… but her success comes at the considerable psychological expense of hoards of impressionable girls, who will spend half their lives hating themselves because they look like ordinary women instead of an overhyped caricature. The makers of Barbie can dress her up in a lab coat or a business suit, but Barbie's purpose has nothing to do with what she wears and everything to do with how she looks. That is her ultimate message to the girls who enter her world: what you do doesn't matter unless you ooze sex appeal while doing it. That means having certain physical attributes, such as unnaturally long legs and huge breasts."

> If Barbie were human, she would be 7 feet tall with a 44-inch bust, 17-inch waist and 40-inch hips.

If Barbie were human, she would be 7 feet tall with a 44-inch bust, 17-inch waist and 40-inch hips.

Again, this is not even close to reality, but we have gotten so far away from what beauty really is. Breast implants are such a normal thing today it's ridiculous; but you can thank Barbie for planting those seeds. Putting silicone in your body is pure insanity! Beauty does not come from the outside! Believe it or not, back in the 1920's A.K.A. the roaring twenties, small breasts were in style and people were having surgery back then to get smaller breasts—again, pure insanity.

After Barbie, we have the cosmetic and hair industries. I have heard a well-known stylist on television say, "I'm going to put this on your hair. That will make it 'look' healthy." Did you catch that? It's not good for your hair, but it will make it look healthy. It's like steroids, which make you look good, but it's horrible for your body. The outside doesn't make you beautiful!

I'm not saying not to wear makeup or style your hair. Cosmetics should be used to enhance your natural beauty, not to create this false you. Also, today's market is demanding more natural and healthy products for your skin and hair. Take advantage of them.

Next, we have magazines. The reality is if you had your own staff of make-up and hair people like these television and movie stars do, then you would look like they do. Most magazines have pictures of all the stars looking perfect. Then if that's not bad enough, there are the ads! With all the airbrushing and Photoshop capabilities, you can literally do anything. You can erase any line or redesign any body part. It's almost comedy when you look at it. It's more like a cartoon to be really honest.

Then we have the television, soap operas, sitcoms and commercials. All of them are just destroying your self-confidence, little by little. Let's start with the commercials.

A lot of it is subconscious. The basic message is that you cannot be beautiful unless you look like this, or smell like this or have this. Try this: the next time your turn on the television, grab a piece of paper and a pen and look at a specific commercial and ask yourself, "what is it telling me?" If you can, record it with your DVR and watch it over and over. Listen to the music, look at the clothes the people are wearing, look at the hair and makeup. The more you study a commercial, the more you will see how ridiculous it is. Write down all the things that are not real about a specific commercial. For example, most women do not have their hair and makeup perfect to

> The more you study a commercial, the more you will see how ridiculous it is.

clean the house. Also, notice the pets in the commercials, always perfectly groomed and clean. See what I mean? It's not reality, but if you not looking for it, you may buy into it, again mostly at a subconscious level.

If the commercials are that bad, then think about the shows themselves. Most women know their daytime soaps and their nighttime soaps like *Desperate Housewives* are pure garbage, but even the regular sitcoms are just as bad. The kids are always rebellious, and the dad is always passive while the mom is the one doing everything. Meanwhile, everyone is insulting everyone and making sly comments, and it's all about tearing down, never building up. The only sitcom that had any quality in my opinion was the *Cosby Show*. Not only was it funny, but you had real morals and a quality family life portrayed. I'm not judging you by your choice in television programs; I'm just saying that if you want to live your dreams, then you need to rethink the input in your life.

Lastly, we have the big monsters: billboards. These are almost worse than the magazines because you can't escape them, and they are larger than life! So here are some things you can do to defend yourself: Move to a part of town with no billboards, like we did. However, living in Los Angeles, we still have to drive to other places, so we can't totally escape them. Here is a great way to displace the negative message of a billboard ad. The mind can only think of one thing at a time, so if you see a billboard that oozes fake beauty, just say to yourself out loud, "I'M BEAUTIFUL." Of course, the first time you do this you will feel uncomfortable, very similar to the first time you did anything. It's like telling your kids, "Oh, walking is not for you," when they are taking their first steps and falling all over the house. So you have to apply some common sense and stick to it. Every time you see a negative billboard just say out loud or to yourself, "I'm beautiful". Imagine bombarding your own mind with the message that you are beautiful every day. The longer you do this, the bigger your self-esteem will grow. Now you don't have to do this, but if you want to build your belief in yourself and live your dreams, then I suggest you take action and do it.

Ok, if you're ready to change, please realize that it's impossible to cleanse yourself of this lifelong brainwashing overnight. I could do it in thirty to ninety days if we took you to a tropical island with no television, cell phones, radio, etc. But let's face it, Madonna was right. We are living in a material world. Where do we find balance? How do we rid ourselves of some of these self-imagine killers?

The secret to pollution is dilution. Start diluting the lie. Start diluting the input. Turn off *Desperate Housewives*. Turn on *What Not to Wear*. Look at real people instead of these women with a staff running around making them look perfect. Turn off the soap operas, and read some quality books. If you do watch a lot of soap operas you will find yourself being very suspicious of your boyfriend or husband when they are late or have to cancel an engagement due to work. You will start thinking they are running off with someone. Also, you will become a huge gossiper with your girlfriends.

I can guarantee that if you turn off the soaps for sixty days, your life will transform. If all you get out of this book is to just do that, then you will be so far ahead in life it will amaze you. Next, cancel all your beauty magazine subscriptions. Purge yourself from this bombardment of false beauty and no reality. I'm not saying it's easy to do; I'm just saying if you want to live your dreams, you have to believe in yourself, and these magazines are stealing your self-image a little bit every day.

Next, when shopping at the grocery store, make sure to check out at a station without the tabloids, if possible. We have full-time staff that does our shopping for us now, but every once in awhile, I will be at the store, and every time I go through the line, I feel polluted. I'm bombarded will all this junk! I want to go home and take a shower and just get it off me. It's similar to people who have quit smoking. Once they really quit, the smell of smoke disgusts them. It will be the same with you. Once you clear your mind and start building yourself image, you will see how much better you feel. Then, when you see one of these magazines or tabloids, you will feel the same way I do. I promise.

> You are in life exactly where you should be because of the way you think.

I know a lot of you readers are having negative thoughts about all my suggestions. You're thinking, "Well, that sounds silly," or "I don't see myself doing that." This is the exact reason you are not living your dreams. You are in life exactly where you should be because of the way you think. If you start to think differently and open your mind, you can start the process of growth. Once you dilute everything, you can start growing and changing and discover your true beauty!

Women are the most beautiful when they know who they are, and they are living their dreams. You won't be able to build your self-belief and live your dream if your mind is cluttered with all this junk you put in it every day. Step by step, cleanse your mind from the junk you're letting influence it. Then, once you're cleansed, we can start the next step of building your self-belief and then begin living your dreams.

TAKE ACTION NOW!

#1. What magazines and television shows are you willing to purge from your life so you can start living your dreams?

#2. Decide today to stop buying the beauty lie and accept that you are perfectly and wonderfully made.

FALSE BELIEFS ABOUT MONEY

CHAPTER 6

Well, since Money is my last name, and I have gone from having none of it to an abundance of it, I'm extra qualified to talk with you about it.

I marvel at all the great stock tips given by people with no money and all the investment opportunities sold by people who have no money. If it were such a great opportunity, why aren't the people taking advantage of it rather than selling it? You need to be very careful who you take your advice from. Make sure they have fruit on the tree! Remember, the title of this book is *Take Action Now: How to Live Your Dreams in Less Than Three Weeks*, not *How to Be a Billionaire*. As of this writing, I have yet to join the billionaire ranks, but rest assured, the second I do, you will see a book by me helping you to do the same.

So let's get down to money in general. Money in itself does two things: it amplifies character, and it gives options. If you have no money, you have no options, and if you're a complete idiot you will just be a giant idiot that is known around the world. Warren Buffett has similar beliefs. He said, "Of the

> Money in itself does two things: it amplifies character, and it gives options.

billionaires I have known, money just brings out the basic traits in them. If they were jerks before they had money, they are simply jerks with a billion dollars."

For example, let's look at Michael Vick for a moment. Here is a guy who had it all. He had NFL fame, his jersey was one of the NFL's best sellers, and he had plenty of disposable income. He was in the middle of a 120 million dollar contract, and that does not include endorsements. Michael Vick became a household name when his lack of character was amplified by his whole dog fighting scandal. The guy lost everything and then some.

We have all heard it said, mostly by people who have no money, that "money doesn't buy happiness," but to truly understand that, you have to have money. It's all about options: where you can live and what size your house is. A bedroom for each of your children is a great option to have. A sports room for you guys, where you put all helmets and cards and jerseys will make your wife so happy. A spare bedroom and bathroom on the other end of the house for when friends come to stay is another great option, not to mention the type of neighborhood or type of schools, etc. It's not about ego or status; it's about options.

The same applies to car options. Sure, it's cool to have custom, one-of-a-kind cars like a Mach 5 or a Batmobile Tumbler or some high-end luxury BMW. But how about having multiple cars so if one breaks down your world doesn't come to a halt? Forget the 740 BMW for now. How about having an SUV, a two-seater for fun, a 4-door sedan, and then a pickup truck for all those times you need one? This way, if a car breaks down, you don't have to take the day off work and deal with car rentals.

"Do you have any idea how much insurance and gas will cost for all those cars?" I can hear you ask. If that thought crossed your mind, it tells me a lot about the way you think. It tells me you have never had abundance; it tells me that you are broke and negative and that your whole world has a meltdown when a seventy dollar alternator

> When you have abundance, you don't think about gas or insurance.

goes out in your car. When you have abundance, you don't think about gas or insurance. You just pay the bill. In fact, you get to the point where you have other people pay your bills. Trust me; this is a dream worth living and I know from experience.

Now, let's look at a few beliefs on money that are holding you back from living your dreams. The first belief is: *I DON'T WANT MONEY BECAUSE OF ALL THE PROBLEMS IT CAUSES.*

Look at your current problems. Would money solve 99.9 percent of them? Money does not cause the problems; lack of character does. When you have money, you get to make different choices, such as where to put it, how to maximize it, and how to protect it. But those are not problems; those are new experiences.

Another false belief is: *I HAVE SEEN PEOPLE WITH MONEY WHO ARE TOTALLY UNHAPPY.*

They would be the same if they were broke. The money just amplifies things like we talked about before. You are doing everyone a disservice by being poor. You are unable to help your family, friends, and charities. By being poor, you're really being selfish. Please note that I'm not talking about dedicating your life to the mission field or to a great cause. In fact, that may be living your dream. So please don't misunderstand me. If you are dedicating yourself to a life of serving others, say like a Mother Teresa, then I would consider you very wealthy indeed. My point is to help you get past all the negative, "lack of" mentality that some of you have about money. I am not judging you by what you do or do not have.

Lastly, this one: *I DON'T' WANT TO BE MONEY MOTIVATED. ALL RICH PEOPLE THINK ABOUT IS MONEY!*

Money is like air—you don't think about it unless you don't have any. Then it's all you think about. Poor people are way more focused on money than wealthy people! Every decision you make is based on money. What time you wake up, where you eat, what time you eat, what car you drive, where you live, what kind of house you have, your hobbies, your friends, etc. The key is not getting money; the key is getting character and wisdom to truly understand money and harness its power. This world needs more wealthy people who have good character! I invite you to join me in becoming one of these people.

> Money is like air—you don't think about it unless you don't have any.

TAKE ACTION NOW!

#1. What false beliefs about money can you identify and let go of?

2. Think about money as a tool instead of a status symbol.

3. Go back and read the dreams you wrote down from chapter #1. Now ask yourself the same lifestyle question as before and see if you would like to change a few things for the better. Would you like to have multiple homes? What would you be driving now? What charities would you be giving to?

KEY #4 ACTION

CHAPTER 7

For my readers that may be thinking I left some things out in the belief section of this book, I understand. You may be looking for more ways to help you believe in yourself. Well, the best way to build your belief is through action!

What made the Rudy story so great was that despite everyone trying to talk him out of his dream of playing for Notre Dame, he got on the bus anyway. He had no idea how he was going to get in, he just took action. Literally, he took a bus to the campus and said to himself, "I don't know how, but I'm going to make it or die trying."

This is similar to my radio show experience except I knew better than to share my dream with negative family members or negative acquaintances. I faded away from all my negative friends at that point in my life. I had no idea how I was going to get on the air, I just started calling radio stations. Just like sailing a sail boat or being a windsurfer, you have to get the sails up and be on the water so you know which way to turn them. So many people

> **SOMEDAY IS TODAY!**

spend their lives "in the harbor," charting their course for Someday Isle. They tell themselves, "Someday, I'll get it. Someday I'll do this. Someday I'll do that." SOMEDAY IS TODAY! *Take action* and the world is yours!

Listen, I understand any captain worth his salt is going to chart his course, prepare for the boat and bring food and water, etc. However, you don't need

> **"The smartest thing you can do to start a company is to actually start the company."**
> **Will Schroter, Founder and CEO of GO Big network**

weeks and months of preparation to just get out of the harbor for a five minute sail. For example, when I started calling the radio stations, that was me just getting out of the harbor

for a few minutes, testing the sails, seeing if we needed any major repairs. I didn't just waltz into the radio station and demand a show. The kind of dream you want to live determines how many five minute or ten minute or one day sailing trips you need to make before you cast off for your dream. The key is ACTION, ACTION, and ACTION! Each small voyage is a belief builder. "The smartest thing you can do to start a company is to actually start the company." Will Schroter, Founder and CEO of GO Big network

Moliere said: "Men are alike in their promises; it is only in their deeds that they differ."

James said it the best: "For just as the body without the spirit is dead, so faith without actions is also dead."[7]

"Well, what if I fail?" you ask.

There are thousands of books on this subject. In fact, John Maxwell's *Failing Forward* is a great book to start with if this is a major issue for you. I can always give you the Thomas Edison light bulb example, where he failed over 10,000 times trying to make it work. However, that story never really did much for me. Here is what I have learned. When you believe and when you *take action*, failure is fertilizer. Yes, it stinks and no, it's not fun, but it sure makes things grow!

Michael Jordan has a poster that talks about how many game winning shots he missed and how many failures he had, but as long as you keep shooting the ball, as in Michael's case, it doesn't matter.

Look, failure hurts. Do not let anyone lie to you and say it doesn't. Let's keep with the sports theme. Look at baseball players. Hall of Famers and All Stars fail 70 percent of the time. When they put up players' batting averages for example, .300 means they strike out or don't get on base 7 out of 10 times. The plus side is that they are paid millions of dollars to do so. The real reason pro athletes are paid so well is because they fail publicly. They are willing to take the heat and scrutiny for not performing well. They are also willing to take the big pay checks. This is true in any arena. If you're the CEO of a big company and you blow it, you have to answer to the stockholders, the media, and the employees. However, the salary level is on par with most pro athletes. So rather than trying to get over this fear of failure, just take action and keep shooting the ball, keep swinging the bat, and keep your dream in front of you. Living the dream is worth the failure. Just make sure to turn it into fertilizer so you can make things grow.

> The real reason pro athletes are paid so well is because they fail publicly.

> Living the dream is worth the failure. Just make sure to turn it into fertilizer so you can make things grow.

This is what taking action does: when (not if) you fail, but when you fail, you simply take action again and learn from your failures. One of the few companies that understand this is Toyota. According to the book *Extreme Toyota* one of the company's core beliefs is that taking action and not succeeding is ok, because doing nothing is worse.

When it comes to failure the best thing you can do is learn from others' failures. Allow me to share one of my biggest blunders with you.

In 2001, I was in an interesting spot. I recently closed one of my businesses down and was offered a position to basically run my own division for a similar company. Yes, it was a "job," which I'm not big on, but I basically had my own world to create and only really had to answer to the owner. As long as he saw profits, my unorthodox ways were tolerated. As you can imagine, dissolution set in pretty fast. What I finally realized was that I'm not a job guy. I'm a founder; I'm a visionary.

One day, one of my sales guys showed me a letter from the fax machine. Keep in mind: mass e-mails and e-mail marketing were just starting out. The fax machine was still king back then. The letter appeared to be from a foreign dignitary, which made sense because the current company I was at did a lot of international business. Everything seemed to jive. The best part was that the letter talked about millions of dollars that needed to be transported out of this person's country. Most of you have caught on to this by now because these bogus e-mails are sent daily. You have seen them: some lonely widow has 80 million dollars she needs to transport out of Africa or some doctor needs to leave his country but is having trouble with the government so he needs your help to receive the money so he can escape the dictatorship. There are many versions and they all raise suspicions but just put yourself in my shoes. I was constantly being frustrated with customs issues with our customers' international orders. In fact, I could not sell to some countries because they could not import our goods. I grew quite intolerant of customs and forms, bureaucracy and paperwork.

I was a fish on the hook. I bought in "hook, line, and sinker," as they say. I flew to Belgium to meet this guy, Dr. Allen Joy. You may have met him too. We went to a few corporate offices and then to a hotel room where I saw, touched, and felt at least 1 million dollars in cash. Unknown to me it was counterfeit, but I had never seen that much cash before. It was hypnotic, and I was dazed. I had to sit down because my head was spinning.

I forked over $65,000 or so of traveler's checks and was told that's what they needed to release the money. By then, I knew something was off, but I didn't care. I saw the money and justified it by saying how much I was going to give to charity, etc.

Long story short, I ended up getting scammed out of $100,000 total. Mind you, it was all borrowed from credit cards and friends. The only thing I got out of it was a pile of fertilizer and two one hundred dollar bills. I had one of those made into a money ring. You may have seen them before. They fold the money into a shape of a ring and then laminate it. Normally, this process is done with a one dollar bill, but I had it done with a one hundred dollar bill, so whenever I wear it, it reminds me of that wonderful learning experience. Now, whenever I take action, that experience is always with me, and I can draw upon it to make better decisions. This is just one of my many blunders. It is better for you to learn from my failure than to make it yourself. You save a lot of money that way.

Taking action does more than just get you moving. In fact, motion is what creates emotion. Let's say you're at a college basketball game at a major university during a big game. There is one second left, and your team makes the game winning shot.

In fact, motion is what creates emotion.

What do you do next? You stand up and cheer. Most of the time, you don't even notice you are standing up. You are just on your feet and excited. Now what if you are rooting for the other team and they just lost? Are you jumping up and down? No. More than likely you are slumped in your chair or if you are standing your head is down. Your motion or movements create your emotional moods.

Try this exercise with me: If you are in your chair, stay seated. If you're in bed, sit up. Ready? Ok, I want you to act depressed. Seriously, just pretend that you are depressed.

Did you notice that your shoulders dropped and you began to slouch? Motion really does create emotion.

Now, jump to your feet or jump out of bed and clap your hands. Did you do it? If you did it, you noticed your depression was gone instantly. You cannot act depressed while you are acting excited.

If you have ever watched a sporting event on television and they showed the players' benches, you can easily tell who is winning without looking at the score. Body language tells you everything. This is why it's important to use motion to your advantage. I know most of you did not jump out of your chair or bed and clap your hands. Why? Because you talked yourself out if it, saying things like, "I just got comfortable, this is crazy, what will my spouse say." This is the same way you have talked yourself out of taking action to live your dreams. If you were one of the few who did jump up, then congratulations! You have taken the next step to making your dreams come true. Let me explain.

The reason people do not take action on living their dreams is because they don't feel like it. Sure, when they are at a seminar or watching a movie like *Rudy* or even reading this book, everything is great. You're feeling good, but then … tomorrow happens, and life gets in the way or you're tired when you get home.

For example, let's say one of your dreams is to write a book, but after a tough day at the office and your garbage disposal goes out and there is a playoff game on television, you just talk yourself out of it, even though you really want to write that book. So, take action, drop, and do two or three push-ups, run in place and clap your hands, sing your alma mater's fight song really loud. If you're a UCLA fan, do an 8 clap (if you don't know what that is it's a UCLA thing). Do something that gets you pumped and moving. This will break your state of laziness or complacency and get you excited to turn on the computer and start writing that book. The type of exercise doesn't matter. It's the motion that matters. Motion creates emotion. You may be able to accomplish this with music as well. Have you ever seen someone in their car just rocking out to a song totally oblivious to the rest of the world? Perhaps someone has seen you do it? The music gets you to move your body which gets you pumped up so you can take action.

Keith Johnstone, Improv theater founder said; "In life, most of us are highly skilled at suppressing action." Use motion to change your mood and to take action on living your dreams.

> "In life, most of us are highly skilled at suppressing action."

TAKE ACTION NOW!

#1. What dream would you live if you were guaranteed not to fail? This is the dream I encourage you to take action on and start living.

2. What type of motion can you use (jumping jacks, clapping hands, etc.) to help you break your current state and *take action*?

High 5's. Gets others going too!

MORE ACTION

CHAPTER 8

The title of this book, *Take Action Now*, is based on the law of diminishing intentions. The longer you wait for something, the colder it gets. We have all heard the saying "Strike while the iron is hot," and it's so true. How many times have you had a great idea in the shower or in your car, but when you get in a place to write it down, it's gone? Then, a few months or even years later, you see your idea on the shelf in a store or on television. This is the worst feeling to ever have.

Take action so you can *take action*! Huh? What do I mean? Well for me, I have pen and paper in my bathroom at all times. Plus, I have dry erase pens so I can even jot things down on the mirror. Many a hit song has been written in fog on the mirror. I also have pen and paper in each of my cars, so I can jot down any idea that comes to mind. I even keep pens and paper in my nightstand so that I can wake up in the middle of the night or right when I'm falling asleep and write down that key idea. Get the pen and paper now so that when you have that next idea, you're not saying, "Man,

I should have put some pen and paper in this drawer."

IDEAS ARE USELESS without the will to act!

So, go get a pen and some scratch paper, and put them in your best idea spots, your shower or wherever. Don't worry, I'll wait while you put the book down and *take action now*.

> IDEAS ARE USELESS without the will to act!

Did you do it? Again, *take action now* and do it!

So, why do our best ideas come to us in the most inconvenient places, like in the shower? Because we are relaxed, because we are simply not thinking and we are able to let go. Isn't it scary how our mind works better when we are not using it? Have you ever tried to remember someone's name, but for the life of you, it just wouldn't come to mind. Then, an hour or two later, the name just pops in your mind without you consciously thinking about it. That's your subconscious mind at work. Let it work for you! Look at ways you can *take action* to do things that relax you.

I recently hired a yoga instructor to come to my house. I don't really like yoga, but it helps me clear my mind and relax, plus it helps some of my old football injuries. So for me, I consciously schedule ahead of time a certain day and hour that I'm going to relax. The best part is after my 1 hour Yoga session I walk back to my office and I get all kinds of great ideas.

Another great thing about *taking action* is that action cures fear.

Going back to the whole motion creates emotion idea, once you start moving or start talking, for example, in the case of giving a speech, the beginning is always the most nerve racking. All professional speakers, even the great ones, have fear before they speak, but they manage that fear by taking action. They practice their intro over and over so that the moment they are introduced and they start into the speech, as each word flows, they get calmer and calmer. One world-class speaker put it this way: "I always have butterflies in my stomach before a speech. I just get the butterflies to fly information." The act of speaking is what cures the fear or the nervousness.

Action also cures excuses. Jackie Robinson said, "Don't complain; just work harder." Notice the work part, *taking action*. Here is

> Jackie Robinson said, "Don't complain; just work harder."

another way to put it. Gas is a huge excuse I see people use that keeps them from taking action. Stop whining about gas prices! If you're not willing to sell your car and walk, you have to buy gas, so it doesn't matter how much it is. So stop complaining and use that energy to take action on living your dreams.

Your body is designed for action. Have you ever had a relative in a nursing home that had a bed sore? Bed sores are from lying in one place too long. It's the old "move it or lose it" principle. Your body was deigned to be put in motion, to move, to be put into action.

"But what if I go in the wrong direction once I take action?" you ask. Simple. Change course, and reset the sail. Do it quickly, though. You don't want to drift off for weeks and months at a time. It's all about making small corrections quickly. Look at airline pilots; they are off course 90 percent of the time. They just keep making small adjustments along the way. Notice that pilots now have air traffic control to talk to and navigation computers to keep them on course. This is why you need a life coach, someone to keep you on course. www. lifecoach5.com is a great way to get world-class, cost-effective life coaching to keep you on course.

I know, this is another plug, but I truly believe in my heart that this site will help you.

They did a study on people over ninety-five years of age and asked them one open-ended question. If you could live your life over again, what would you do differently? The two main answers were: 1. Do more things that would live on after they die, and 2. they said they would risk more. We don't always get what we want, but we always get what we choose! Choose to *take action*!

> We don't always get what we want, but we always get what we choose!

As we wrap up this chapter, some of you may be a little resistant to some of my ideas and you may even be thinking, "Does this guy think he has all the answers?"

The answer is YES!

For the most part, everyone knows the answers! How many times have you said, "I know I shouldn't be eating this" or "I know I need to forgive so and so" or "Wow, someone should help that person." The answer is action! *Take action* on what you know you should be doing.

My wife and I took this idea and applied it to our marriage in a way some would say is extreme. We decided in our first year of marriage that we would renew our vows in a different state or country every year. Every time we tell someone about this tradition, all married people say, "Wow, that is cool. I should do that," but they never do. See, we take action on things that we know will benefit our marriage. Now if this is something you would like to do but you're getting all uptight about how much it's going to cost, hold on. Just keep it simple and fun. A lot of the times, the ceremonies are very small. We don't buy a big wedding gown each year; in fact, one year we did it at the Excalibur hotel in Las Vegas. They provided us with a King and Queen outfit, and we had a blast. It can just be the two of you in some little country church or on the beach. The size and location is irrelevant. It is the action of physically renewing our commitment to each other. That is so powerful. The key is that we take action and do it.

> The key is that we take action and do it.

Before this chapter ends, I have one last live your dream story for you that is a perfect example of the benefits of taking action. Thanks to the hit movie *Batman Begins* and the sequel *The Dark Knight*, the

Batman franchise has been reborn. However, back in 1989, Tim Burton made the first inroads with his Batman movie starring Michael Keaton, Jack Nicholson, and Kim Basinger.

In 1989, I was nineteen and living at home with my older brother and we were huge Batman fans. We heard about the movie coming out, and we planned to dress me up as the Joker for the premiere in Hollywood. Now, we had a budget of fewer than twenty dollars, but we didn't let that stop us. We went to a thrift store and bought a white suit and dyed it purple. Then, we took a Sharpie pen and drew the "pinstripes" on the jacket and pants. Believe it or not, the suit looked pretty good.

The next day, I dyed my hair green and then the fun began. My brother wanted to be a Hollywood makeup artist at one time, so he experimented on me. He made me a latex narrow chin and cheek bones and then glued them to my face. Then, we put on the white makeup, lipstick, and voila! Off to Hollywood and the Mann's Chinese theater we went.

As you can imagine, the place was packed, and we got a lot of attention. The Mann's Chinese theater even dressed up one of their employees as the Joker; however they didn't really go all out. He came up to me and smiled and said, "Wow." I put my hand out to shake his. I had one of those hand buzzers in it, and he jumped about five feet. He laughed and then just walked away, shaking his head knowing he was out-classed.

The only bummer of the night was the theater was sold out long before we got there. We were bummed, but we were O.K. with not making it in until a suspicious man came up to me and said, "Hey, you want to get in?" My brother and I jumped at the chance, and then he asked the magic question. "How much you got"? Well, I think the guy figured out we didn't have the funds he was looking for, but he liked the whole costume, and I think he felt sorry for us.

After we gave him every cent we had, which was maybe thirty-five bucks, he had us sit down near the door next to a high-end couple. When the usher came, I was fully expecting to have him boot us out, but to my surprise, he said, "Right this way." He took us upstairs to a VIP section with a balcony. My brother and I were literally in shock, we were so excited. What capped the night was when I leaned over the balcony and looked down and a few people started to point and stare. Pretty soon, more people started looking and pointing, and the whole theater broke out into cheers and a standing ovation for me, the "Joker." I smiled and waved and played it up as much as I could. It was literally a Hollywood dream come true. All because my brother and I didn't just talk about how cool it would be, we *took action*.

TAKE ACTION NOW!

#1. What one thing can you take action on right now that will start you on the road to living your dreams?

#2. If you are married or in a serious relationship, take action via a note or flowers or set up a vow renewal to let your significant other know how much you love them.

#3. Go back and read the dreams you wrote down from chapter 1. Now ask yourself the same lifestyle question as before and dwell on it for a moment. Where would you live? What would you be driving? What types of activities and trips would you be taking?

KEY # 5 TODAY

CHAPTER 9

Today is all you have. Too many people get intimidated with starting something new or simply just changing. But here is the secret. All you need to do is just work on today. For example, consider Michael Phelps, who won eight gold medals in the historic 2008 Olympics in China. Most people think he trained for four years, and that is simply not true. He made a choice to train today! He cannot train a day in advance. He can't say, "Oh, I think I'll train for Tuesday and Wednesday since I'm already here. Michael Phelps, Michael Jordan or any great athlete have this in common with you, they can only train today.

> Michael Phelps, Michael Jordan or any great athlete have this in common with you, they can only train today.

Let's look at diets. People say, "Oh my gosh, I have to survive this diet for two weeks!" Not true. You just have to make good food choices today! That's it. It's a one-day diet plan. (In case you are wondering, I'm already writing that book).

See how simple this is? Just make a decision that today you will change, today you will make a better food choice, today you will take a walk around the block. Today, Today, Today! Remember the saying "An apple a day keeps the doctor away?" What if it's true? In today's world, we have it confused. It's the latte a day or the donut a day. As the legendary Jim Rohn would say, if you confuse the apple a day with the donut a day, it's a recipe for disaster.

What you do today is so critical because it's the only day you have.

John Wooden, the greatest college basketball coach of all time was really big on this. He would get after his players for not giving 100 percent in practice. He would explain that they couldn't make it up tomorrow. You cannot give more that 100 percent, so if you give 75 percent today, you cannot give 125 percent tomorrow. It's lost. Today is all you have.

Just in case your memory is not as sharp as it used to be, this daily belief that Wooden instilled in his players led him to ten NCAA Championships in twelve years, winning seven of those in a row. People get all excited about a back-to-back win. HA! Try seven wins in a row and ten wins in twelve years. It's safe to say those records will stand forever!

"You will never change your life until you change something daily"- John Maxwell. This statement is so true. Everyone thinks change is some big process. Like quitting smoking, you don't need to quit smoking forever. In fact, you can't. You can only not smoke today. The same applies to alcohol, internet porn, or any addiction. You can never quit drinking or porn forever; just don't give in to the addiction today. See how the pressure comes off you? You're just making a choice to not smoke today.

> "You will never change your life until you change something daily"- *John Maxwell.*

You are exactly where you should be in life because of the way you think. If you look at change as a daily decision, you can make the decision to start living your dream today. "So how does that work exactly?" some of you may be asking.

O.K., let's say you dream of becoming a fashion designer. Currently, you're working at Home Depot and you have no fashion schooling. Where do we go from here?

Day 1: After you wake up, decide to ask yourself this question. "What will I do today to get me closer to being a successful fashion designer?"

Since this is going to be a question you want to ask yourself daily, you will need to create reminders that will force you to ask it. You may want to put a sign on your mirror or on the fridge. You can even put a sign on the toilet seat that says "if you're going to go, go be a fashion designer" or something like that.

I can already hear you say, "but my friends/roommate/ spouse will laugh at me." First off, anyone who is living his or her dream will not laugh. In fact, they will say, "I didn't know you wanted to be a fashion designer. How can I help?" But now you're going to tell me that my friends/roommate/spouse aren't living their dreams. Yes, I know. If this is the case, it is time to reread the association chapter in this book. Remember that when you start living your dream, that non-supportive person will be your number one fan. Like I said before, you owe it to them to live your dream so they can be freed by your light.

O.K., so we have set up some kind of a system that will daily remind us to ask the all-important question: What will I do today to get me closer to being a successful fashion designer?

Day 2: Ask the question and *take action*. Today you may decide to pick up every fashion magazine you can get your hands on so that you can start making a collage board.

Day 3: Ask the question and *take action*. You may decide to buy the supplies to make the collage and start cutting out pictures.

Day 4: Ask the question and *take action*. Are you getting the idea? You take small steps or big steps. The key is to start walking. Let's fast forward to day 7.

Day 7: Ask the question and *take action*. Research online if there are any fashion designers, big or small, in your town. You may be surprised at what you find. You may also discover some fashion designer blogs and websites you never knew existed.

Day 14: Ask the question and *take action*. After blogging with a current designer online and forming a relationship, you ask if this person could mentor you. Perhaps they could review your drawings or look at some of the things you have made. To your surprise they say yes.

Day 21: Ask the question and *take action*. It turns out you get an e-mail from your mentor saying the last design you sent was awesome, and they would like to buy it. You are now starting to live your dream.

The time frame could be three weeks, like I just laid out, or it could be three years. The amount of time it takes is irrelevant; the fact is that you're *taking action* and daily moving towards living your dreams. The more forgiveness you have, the better associations you have, the bigger your belief, and the more action you take will determine the speed of how fast you live your dreams.

You may even discover that after five years you're ready for change and you want to live a new dream. That's O.K.. Life is all about change. Just look at the seasons. Where I live we have summer which is eighty to ninety degrees and then winter which is sixty-five to eighty degrees. But in most parts of the world you have summer, spring, fall and winter. Life is about change and growth. Change and growth all happen on a daily basis. "Don't let

> "Don't let someone else create your world, for when they do they always create it too small."
> *Edwin Louis Cole*

someone else create your world, for when they do they always create it too small." Edwin Louis Cole

If you look at most billionaires, they have a lot going on. Donald Trump has his golf courses, commercial and residential real estate, and his television show, just to name a few. Sir Richard Branson has Virgin Galactic, Virgin Mobile, Virgin America, Virgin Radio, etc. So, don't ever question if it's O.K. to branch off in a new direction regardless of what others say. Again, it's about change and growth. The reason you are not living your dreams yet is because you need to change and grow.

Speaking of growth, did you ever notice that humans are the only form of life on this planet that doesn't grow to their maximum potential? Think about it. Take a tree, for example. Trees dig and stretch their roots as far down as they can go so that they grow as high as they can. Have you ever heard the saying that a fish will grow as big as the tank is? So why do we humans not grow to our potential? Well, the simple fact is our creator gave us the gift of choice. Every day we have a choice. In our home, with our children, we talk about choosing to be "a winner and a giver not a loser and a taker." It's a daily choice. Remember this one? How do you eat an elephant? One bite at a time. It's your choice daily to take that bite, so to speak.

I think what throws people off about this whole "Today is all you have" notion or as John Wooden says, "Make everyday your masterpiece," is that it sounds really simple. Look, all great things are simple. Just ask one of the wealthiest people in the world, Warren Buffett, who says, "The business schools reward difficult complex behavior more than simple behavior, but simple behavior is more effective." This is one of the reasons I kept this book short and simple. Sure, I could fill page after page expanding on many of the ideas I have shared in his book. But I prefer to keep it simple so people like you can instantly apply what you have read and live your dreams faster.

> "Make everyday your masterpiece,"
> *John Wooden*

Another reason today is so critical is because we all know firsthand what happens if we do not take action today. How many of you have started a workout regimen only to drift away from it? One day turns into two, then four, and

> "The business schools reward difficult complex behavior more than simple behavior, but simple behavior is more effective."
> *Warren Buffett*

then pretty soon it's been a month and then a year. Why is it so easy to not take action? Perhaps it is the lack of immediate consequences.

Let's take the donut a day verses the apple a day example. Our bodies are so amazing and so good at survival that you can eat donuts instead of apples for years. But just like a car that you don't take care of, one day, it just goes boom! Your body is the same way. Little by little, you start to feel worse and worse, but not enough to keep you from working, raising a family, etc. Then, before you know it, you're in the hospital and you have major issues. Worse yet, you don't have any "issues" at all because your life has ended. I don't need to give you examples. You know plenty of people who have had major issues or even just suddenly died from not making good daily choices about health.

The same applies to living your dreams. If you continue to make poor daily decisions about money, about personal growth or lack of it, one day you will wake up with a mess on

> Living your dreams is a daily process.

your hands. In fact, most of you reading this are in that mess or hopefully starting to clean it up. Living your dreams is a daily process. The key word is "process"; too many people underestimate the process because of our instant gratification world. Daily, we are bombarded with "overnight" success stories in all areas: sports, entertainment, and the financial world. The typical overnight success has been in the making for years by choosing quality daily decisions that you don't see. This is what got them in a position to become "overnight" wonders.

Some of you reading this book have been making good daily decisions about money and personal growth. Now, with the ideas and things I have shared in this book, you are ready to take action and become that "overnight" success by living your dream, perhaps in less than three weeks.

Today is the day to start living your dreams. Forget about tomorrow; today is the day. Take action and the world is yours!

TAKE ACTION NOW!

#1. Decide what dream you will start to live today.

#2. Ask yourself: "What can I do today that will bring me closer to living the dream of _____ _____.

#3. *Take action* and set up a system so you can ask yourself this question every day.

PUTTING IT ALL TOGETHER

CHAPTER 10

Now that we have gone over each of the 5 keys, let's make sure each one is on your key ring and ready to be put to use, allowing you to live your dreams. As of this writing, I have a very big meeting next week that will secure my ownership in an Arena Football Team. Now I will be the first to tell you that this dream has taken more than three weeks, but this journey has all been worth it. I would like to show you how I used each of the 5 keys to live this dream.

When my bride and I bought our first house the mortgage rep came by my office and saw all my Arena Football paraphernalia. It turns out he is a huge fan as well and we ended up getting our season tickets to the LA Avengers next to each other. As our friendship matured, this man came to me for relationship advice because he saw the great marriage I had and he saw how I used <u>forgiveness</u> first hand with my father and the contractor I talked about earlier. I chose to <u>associate</u> with this man because he and I agreed on certain core values. He is about 15 years my senior and a bachelor so our lifestyles were quite different, however I made it a point to schedule a lunch with him here and there and made sure we connected on the phone and e-mail. As it turned out, this man became an owner of an Arena Football team and he would share with me the ins and outs of ownership. Because I <u>believed</u> that one day I would own my own team, I paid close attention to every detail he shared. As it turned out, he started to have issues with his other partners and I was there to share his pain. Since I have a high belief in myself, I was able to encourage and believe in him through the dark times he was having. Remember you cannot give what you do not have, so if you do not believe in yourself you cannot inspire others to believe in themselves. I also took <u>action</u> and planted seeds about my goals and dreams to buy a portion of the team and help him rid himself of the "bad apples" in the ownership group. This man also saw the action I took in my other enterprises and the success I created, as well as the failures I was able to use as fertilizer to ongoing success. Because <u>today</u> was all I had to work with I did not wait until I had millions in my bank account to discuss ownership options. I talked with this man about the value I could add as a partner to this team.

As it turned out, I shared my dream with this man about being a 7 year old kid who longed to play pro football, but who never really had a shot. The only chance at glory would be to buy a team so I could play in one game. Rather than making it all about me, I showed him the benefits of marketing my story to bring more P.R. to the team. He loved the idea and is now willing to sell me a portion of the team, so not only will I be living the dream as an owner, but I will finally live the dream I had since I was 7 about playing professional football.

Now it is time to start living your dreams! The more forgiveness you have, the better associations you choose, the bigger your belief and the more action you take today, will determine the dreams you will live. Remember, your life is an occasion, rise to it.

This book is just the beginning if you're serious about living your dreams. Allow me to help you with your journey with my #1 online Life Coaching web site www.lifecoach5.com . As an author and speaker I can only do so much; this site is the next step to keep on track to living your dreams. For the highly qualified, I also offer personal coaching that will transform your finances, health and relationships. I look forward to working with you.

END NOTES

1. God's Word Translation

2. The Tipping Point

3. The Tipping Point

4. American King James

5. International Standard

6. World English Bible

7. International Standard James 2:26